To

_____

from

_____

When You Need a Good LAUGH

Phil Callaway

Photography by Kevin Rivoli

H™

HARVEST HOUSE PUBLISHERS
EUGENE, OREGON

When you need a good laugh

Photography copyright © 2013 by Kevin Rivoli

Text copyright © 2013 by Phil Callaway (Weight: 174; Eyes: blue; Hair: formerly blond; Height: 5'11" less one inch for each coming decade; Allergies: jalapeno peppers; Hands: perfect for playing piano if he would have practiced like his mother told him to; Golf Handicap: rising. For more information about Phil Callaway, visit his website, www.laughagain.org.)

Published by Harvest House Publishers
Eugene, Oregon 97402
www.harvesthousepublishers.com

ISBN 978-0-7369-4736-7

Design and production by Koechel Peterson & Associates, Inc., Minneapolis, Minnesota

Harvest House Publishers has made every effort to trace the ownership of all poems and quotes. In the event of a question arising from the use of a poem or quote, we regret any error made and will be pleased to make the necessary correction in future editions of this book.

Printed in China

13 14 15 16 17 18 19 / LP / 10 9 8 7 6 5 4 3 2 1

*To my ever-lovin' daughter and loyal assistant, Rachael,
without whose constant companionship, advice, and encouragement,
this book would have been completed six months earlier.*

PHIL CALLAWAY

For my wife, Michele, and sons, Jack and Nick.

KEVIN RIVOLI

Laughing Matters

THE SHOPPING MALL STALKER

Laughter. What a lifesaver!

My friends Kurt and Lynn were strolling through a busy mall one Saturday. Like most married couples, their wish lists differed, so they agreed to part and then rendezvous in two hours. At the agreed-upon time, Lynn spied Kurt ambling toward their meeting spot. A grin tugged at the corners of her mouth. Stealing up behind him like a guided missile, she pounced upon his back, clamped her legs about his waist, and bit him—a little too hard—on the neck.

Unfortunately it wasn't Kurt.

Unfortunately I am not making this up.

Lynn had few options at this point in her life. She tried to explain herself, but the words were jumbled. She tried to run, but her feet were frozen like in those childhood dreams where the Communists are chasing you. The poor, traumatized, and joyless man saw no humor in it. He turned and fled, leaving Lynn standing there, the focal point of a sellout crowd of shoppers.

Then the most glorious thing happened. Kurt arrived to listen wide-eyed. Bad decisions make great stories, don't they? Standing in that crowded mall, two grownups began to laugh. They laughed like little kids until they couldn't stand up straight. Departing through automatic doors, Lynn leaped onto her husband's back and bit him playfully on the neck. This time there was no doubt. She had the right guy.

Laughter. What a lifesaver! I know of no stronger medication to help wage war on embarrassment, stress, discouragement, fear—maybe even death itself (unless you're diabetic, then insulin is rather important).

5

Children love to laugh. Ka-thwack your head on a tree branch, and they'll love you forever. Slip on the ice, and they'll offer you your own sitcom. But by the time we're a little older, many of us sacrifice the gift of laughter on the altar of maturity. We still want to laugh, but life sucks it out of us. Work. Deadlines. In-laws. Pimples.

I began to lose my laugh back in fifth grade. That was the year grown-ups began to snarl at me. "Smarten up! Wise up! Listen up! Sit up! Stand up! Pick that up! Wash up! Speak up! Shut up! Grow up!" As if I wasn't confused enough, they'd add, "Quiet down! Simmer down! Settle down! Slow down! Get down from there!"

I deserved it. But since when does growing up mean we have to grow cranky? Since when does growing up mean we have to look like we make a living sucking buttons off sofas?

We all agree that life gets serious, that tough times are upon us. That's why I'm a firm believer in making laughter a part of our daily schedule—like sleep, exercise, and our mandatory naps here at home. But how do we keep a laugh handy when the world around us hides them like Easter eggs?

This little book holds five secrets guaranteed to help you say good riddance to the joy suckers. If the laughter has faded from your life, your workplace, or your home, that is about to change.

For twenty years it has been my privilege to entertain audiences with humor. Anyone who does this knows that there are few thrills as exhilarating as watching folks slide from chairs lubricated with a glorious jolt of laughter. I have come to believe that a laugh is something deep inside us trying to shout, "Hey! It's okay! Everything's gonna be fine!"

And it will be okay.

Just ask Lynn and Kurt and the stranger in the mall with an unforgettable story, which I hope he tells his grandchildren one day. Like this book, a story like that should bring a little laughter wherever it goes.

We childproofed the house,
but they keep getting back in.

A friend has this on her voicemail: "I'm not available right now, but thanks for your call. I am making some changes in my life. Please leave a message. If I do not return your call, you are one of the changes."

It is impossible to overestimate the importance of friendship as a spark plug for laughter. A recent study found that people rarely laugh alone but are six times as likely to laugh in the presence of another and thirty times more likely to laugh when in a group. Like a yawn, laughter is contagious. You can get a chuckle from jokes and video clips on the Internet but not the powerful rib-tickling, knee-slapping, fall-over laughter you get when it bounces off others. What helps you laugh? For me it's my kids, my marriage, even my dog.

I got a hamster for my son. It was a pretty good trade.

When our kids were small, we begged them to finish their peas. They became teenagers, and they finished their peas alright. They cleaned their plates. They cleaned *our* plates. They cleaned out the fridge, the pantry, the freezer—everything but the dishwasher. They wouldn't touch that.

Ah, kids. We spend the first two years of their lives teaching them to walk and talk and the next sixteen telling them to sit down and be quiet. When they were small, we held them close and prayed they'd stop screaming and sleep through the night. Then they got to be teenagers, and we couldn't wake them up. They were in the prime sleeping years of their lives. Our son Jeffery slept a world record consecutive twenty-three hours when he was fifteen. I said to my wife, Ramona, "That's not sleeping. That's a coma."

9

When they were young, we put them in a grocery cart and wheeled them into the store. We tried to switch carts with others; they wouldn't take our cart. Older people shuffled over and said, "You think things are bad now! You just wait. Soon they're gonna wanna date and drive your car. Be worried. Be very worried."

Then they shuffled off to the prune and bran flake aisle.

When the kids entered the teen years, those people were back. "It's gonna get worse," they threatened. "You just wait."

I said, "No, I'm not gonna wait. I'm going to enjoy what I have now. Sure, I spend my days following teenagers around the house shutting lights off. I've spent my last fifteen birthdays pretending I like plaid ties and soap-on-a-rope. I carry pictures where my money used to be. But I'm not going to wait. Today is all I get, so I'll make the most of it."

> **"Be merciful to me, O God, for men hotly pursue me."**

Our daughter pasted the Bible verse "Be merciful to me, O God, for men hotly pursue me" (Psalm 56:1) to her door when she was sixteen. Now she's in her twenties and finally let a boy catch her. They were married one year ago.

Our son came in one night and said, "Mom, I'd like to bring in three girls, and you have to guess which one I'm going to marry." Sure enough, he paraded three gorgeous girls into the living room. They conversed with my wife, and finally he said, "Okay, that's enough. Guess, Mom. Which one is it?"

Ramona pointed at the one in the middle. "Her!"

"Wow, how did you know?"

She said, "I don't like her."

The truth is we love this gal. And now that they're married, we love going to their house and doing things they used to do at our place. We flip lights on, leave the front door open when it's minus twenty, and put an open jar of mayo on the counter and leave it there overnight. We let taps drip and replace their Michael Bublé CDs with something from Pat Boone—and crank it up. Best of all, we love to sit on their sofa…and neck.

Now we're going to be grandparents! We don't know when, but you never know.

MAN'S BEST FRIEND

How could I mention friendship without telling you about my dog, Mojo II? I think the friendliest being in all the world is Mojo when she's wet. We paid $300 for this dog, or $100 per brain cell. When she's chewing on a bone and I happen by, she snarls. Does she think I want the bone, that I'll put it between my paws and gnaw on it?

Still, dog is man's best friend. If you doubt me, try a little experiment. Lock your wife and your dog in the bathroom for about an hour. When you open the door, see who's glad to see you.

No medication on earth is more effective than a puppy licking your face. Helen Thomson said, "A well-trained dog will make no attempt to share your lunch. He will just make you feel so guilty that you cannot enjoy it."

WISDOM FOR LIFE

- Don't jump from the train when you're in a tunnel.

- Never leave a room during a committee meeting. You'll be elected.

- A person who is nice to you but rude to the waiter is not a nice person.

- Behind every successful man is a woman. And behind every unsuccessful man, there are two.

- See no evil, hear no evil, date no evil.

- Avoid parking tickets by leaving your windshield wipers on full speed.

- It's always darkest before dawn. So if you're going to steal your neighbor's newspaper, that's the time to do it.

- A true gentleman is a man who can play the accordion but doesn't.

- Remember: In just two days, tomorrow will be yesterday.

We learn much from our canine companions—loyalty, forgiveness, perseverance, and to turn around three times before going to sleep. My mother once said, "Every boy who has a dog should also have a mother, so the dog can be fed regularly."

Will there be dogs in heaven? When my very first dog, Mojo I, died, my wise old minister father answered my question this way: "According to the Bible, there are animals in heaven, son. And remember, God only threw the humans out of the Garden of Eden."

THE PRINCESS AND THE CHEAPSKATE

I heard on the radio that diamonds are a girl's best friend. It's a little disappointing. I thought men were. On a list of women's passions, guys finished number three. The winner? Chocolate. Second place? Cats. I thought God created cats to show that not everything on earth has a purpose. Apparently not.

Ramona and I have been married thirty years, and I'm still learning new things about her. She admitted recently that she cleans the house faster when she's mad at me. All this time I thought she was just superefficient. When she's really mad, she cleans the toilet.

"How does that help, honey?" I asked.

"I use your toothbrush."

Just kidding. But ours is a miracle marriage. We're so different. I'm punctual. She's late. In ct her relatives arrived on the *Juneflower*. She's generous. I'm cheap. I critiqued her once r only getting one cup of tea from a teabag. "My mom used to use one teabag for weeks," I id. "Then she'd make soup with it. And a couple salads. We'd floss with the string. Then my ends and I would smoke the leftovers."

Miraculously she loves me. She even got me a GPS unit for Christmas. If you don't have e yet, you really should. You can now have a woman in your car telling you where to go! metimes you hear, "Turn left in one mile. Quit fiddling with the CD player. Turn left in quarter mile. Quit picking your nose. You missed your turn. Recalculating. I told you so." his is the closest I will ever come to polygamy—two women in my car telling me where to . It poses a dilemma. What do you do if the two women disagree? Listen to your wife, even you're lost for weeks. That's why happily married men are discarding GPS units out win- ws everywhere. Don't buy one. Just find a ditch somewhere and load up.

Here are a few other Guaranteed Marriage Savers (GMS) from a guy who's learned the rd way:

- Remember her birthday. Forget her age.
- Don't let the sun go down on your wrath. Stay up and fight.

13

- Remember the ancient Chinese marriage secret: "Wash face in morning. Neck at night."
- Avoid using the following phrases: "You have too many shoes already." "Crying is blackmail." "Shopping is not a sport." "Honey, the playoffs are on. Can we talk about this during the ads?"
- Don't eat garlic unless she does.
- Just once try these words: "That's fascinating. Tell me more." "I made some mutton curry with oregano. I hope that sounds okay." "I know. Let's go get you some shoes."
- Laugh lots. Even when she says, "If you want breakfast in bed, sleep in the kitchen."
- Every four to six years, whether you need to or not, buy underwear in bulk.
- If you're a gal, try these words: "Brad Pitt's got nothing on you." "Is there anything you can't fix?" "Here's the remote control. Let's watch something violent."
- Read a book to her. One of mine! What a blessing!
- Dance together—even if your children are around and make gagging noises.
- Discuss the bills after the other's eaten.
- Love even when you don't feel like it.
- Romance her. Better to kiss your wife goodbye when you leave the house than kiss your house goodbye when you leave your wife.
- Be grateful you have each other.
- Pray together.
- Look for the good in each other…and always find it.
- Tighten jars. That way she will need you more.

Every single day I can't believe this gorgeous woman married me. She shares my address and often my pillow. She has seen me at my worst, and still she loves me. And though I have to hide my toothbrush, the number one reason we're still together is grace—the grace of a woman whose age I can't remember and of a God who loves us both.

*Dress in the wardrobe
God picked out for you:
compassion, kindness,
humility, quiet strength,
discipline. Be even-tempered,
content with second place,
quick to forgive an offense.
Forgive as quickly and
completely as the Master
forgave you.*

*And regardless of what
else you put on, wear love.
…Never be without it.*

COLOSSIANS 3:12-14 MSG

AMBUSHING THE JOY SUCKERS

*I worry that the guy who invented rap music
is out there working on something new.*

I once asked the famous author and radio preacher Chuck Swindoll what he takes the most flack for. "Humor," he said. Though many tell him that his laugh is the only one they hear in their homes, others want him to stop. "How do you deal with their jabs?" I asked. "Some people want you to be as miserable as they are," he responded, "and I'm not getting on that bus." Amen! The trip seems never-ending when we travel with the self-appointed guardians of misery.

Have you met sour people whose faces are cemented in a downward scowl? Genetics didn't help them, but chances are they've been sampling at least one of the following forbidden prunes.

What? Me worry?

Do you ever worry? I do. I worry about potholes, cell phone radiation, oversleeping, and getting frisked at airports. You say, "Don't worry. Be happy." I say, "Are you crazy? There's so much to worry about nowadays." Take email. Please take it. I've had enough. Here's information I've found in my inbox alerting me to emergencies I had no idea I needed to worry about:

- KFC chickens are mutants.
- Cold water causes cancer.
- Mr. Clean Magic Erasers contain formaldehyde.
- If you go to sleep at a party, you could wake up without a kidney.
- Shop at a mall, and you may be drugged with a perfume sample.
- Never ever pick up a five dollar bill in a parking lot. Someone might be lurking beneath your car to grab your leg.

17

We all know that worry is like a porch swing. It gives you something to do but never takes you anywhere. Still we worry about being underpaid, overtaxed, and underappreciated.

If chronic worry is pulverizing your complexion and ulcerizing your kidneys, the cure is closer than you think. Don't skim over this. Read it slowly. It has the power to change your life. Ready? "Don't fret or worry. Instead of worrying, pray. Let petitions and praises shape your worries into prayers, letting God know your concerns. Before you know it, a sense of God's wholeness, everything coming together for good, will come and settle you down" (Philippians 4:6-7 MSG).

Each time worry arrives, show it through the door of prayer. The more we pray, the less we panic.

Feed your mind on things that are honorable, pure, lovely, and of good report. They're seldom in the newspaper or on TV. They are waiting to be discovered in the pages of good books and the words of good friends. Default to rejoicing at every opportunity, and your life will be transformed. No lie. You'll find that the God who has shown up for saints throughout history is not about to abandon you.

So rejoice, relax, and reflect on God's goodness. Hang out with positive people. Read that book of cartoons.

osen your tie. Hug a friend's Chihuahua. Share a joke with a friend. Lighten up and laugh.

And read emails sometimes. One just arrived that should fix my worries. Bill Gates is sending me $150,000.

m not bitter; I just don't like you.

Life offers plenty of opportunity to court bitterness. When one friend ticked me off, I remember thinking, *May your children be blessed with musical giftedness—on the bagpipes. May ur stereo play CDs loud and clear—but only ones by Barry Manilow.*

Ever felt that way? Is there someone you'd like to see have immovable biker gang tenants? he initial rush of bitterness almost makes it worthwhile having enemies. It provides a cer-in satisfaction for a time. But for every day you are bitter, you lose twenty-four hours of joy. nd soon you'll hear the sucking sound of laughter draining from your life.

"Hey," you say, "I'm angry and it's justified." I'm sure it is.

Anger says, "This is wrong. It needs to stop."

Bitterness says, "If the front wheel falls off his bicycle, I'll throw a party."

As with worry, there's a cure, of course. It will take an act of the will, but even more, an act f love. Here it is: "Make a clean break with all cutting, backbiting, profane talk. Be gentle vith one another, sensitive. Forgive one another as quickly and thoroughly as God in Christ orgave you" (Ephesians 4:31-32 MSG). The trouble with giving in to bitterness is that you ecome the very thing you disdain. Bitterness does three things to you. It claps you in irons, ements your frown, and contradicts the behavior God showed you.

How can a bitter person pray honestly, "Forgive us our debts as we forgive our debtors?" Tim Keller is right: "An unforgiving heart is an unforgiven heart." When bitterness creeps up on me, I am reminded that I follow a man whose first words amid blood, horror, and his hands nailed to wood were "Father, forgive." To the degree we remember what Jesus has done for us—to that degree we can forgive.

Sometimes this means forgiving ourselves. I've had to forgive myself for doing dumb stuff. Falling off a stage in front of an audience. Forgetting a punch line on national television.

Dropping barbells on my nose (I'd rather not talk about it). Lewis B. Smedes wrote, "Forgiving what we cannot forget creates a new way to remember. We change the memory of our past into a hope for our future."

Forgiveness and love blow the doors off the prison of bitterness and free us up to laugh agai

Just because you're paranoid doesn't mean they won't get you.

There are benefits to paranoia. These include high blood pressure, irritability, itchiness, heartburn, late nights, and gas. Has any culture experienced more paranoia than ours? The emails keep arriving:

- Never combine shrimp and vitamin C. This causes death.
- The bottom of a woman's purse has more bacteria than a toilet seat.
- Avoid sitting on hotel bedspreads.
- Don't open a public bathroom door without using a paper towel.
- Hold your cell phone only to the left ear. Right ear usage directly affects the brain.

This reminds me of the answering machine message: "If you are paranoid, stay on the line. We're tracing the call."

Fear can be a healthy thing. For some, fear of jail is the beginning of wisdom. Fear of lung cancer helped a friend kick a pack-a-day habit. Fear of licking metal doorknobs in winter has kept my tongue intact since that fateful day in January of 1965.

When the Moscow Circus came to New York, a fearless and beautiful lion tamer performed an astonishing feat. She walked into the cage of a fierce lion and headed straight toward it. The lion humbly wrapped its paws around her and nuzzled her with affection as the crowd thundered its approval. All cheered except for one farmer who hollered, "What's so great about that? Anybody can do that!" The ringmaster laughed. "If you'd like to try, step into the cage." The farmer replied, "Sure. But first get that lion out of there."

If you're climbing over a zoo fence late at night, it's good to fear lions. But fear gives small things big shadows. It chokes courage, stunts joy, clamps us in a headlock, and gives us noogies. We fear that next round of layoffs. Terrorism. The future. Loneliness. Flying. Death. Public speaking. Some fear string (linonophobia) or the great mole rat (zemmiphobia).

Big Screen Smiles

~ee Amigos

~ican girl: *"Which one do you like?"*

~men (Patrice Martinez): *"I like the one that's ~so smart."*

~xican girl: *"Which one is that?"*

Finding Nemo

Dory (Ellen DeGeneres):
*"I suffer from short term memory loss. It runs in my family...
At least I think it does."*

~rplane

~. Barry Rumack (Leslie Nielsen): *"Can you fly this plane, and land it?"*

~d Striker (Robert Hays): *"Surely you can't be serious."*

~. Barry Rumack: *"I am serious... And don't call me Shirley."*

~ Good As It Gets

~. Green (Lawrence Kasdan):
"~ you want to see me, you will ~ do this. You will make an ~pointment."

~elvin Udall (Jack Nicholson):
~r. Green, how can you diagnose ~meone as an obsessive compulsive ~sorder, and then act like I have ~me choice about barging in here?"

The Pink Panther Strikes Again

Inspector Clouseau (Peter Sellers):
"I thought you said your dog did not bite."

Innkeeper: *"That's not my dog."*

Princess Bride

Vizzini (Wallace Shawn): *"I can't compete with you physically, and you're no match for my brains."*

Man in Black (Cary Elwes): *"You're that smart?"*

Vizzini: *"Let me put it this way. Have you ever heard of Plato, Aristotle, Socrates?"*

Man in Black: *"Yes."*

Vizzini: *"Morons."*

Ace Ventura

Ace Ventura (Jim Carrey):
"If I'm not back in five minutes...just wait longer!"

What About Bob

Dr. Leo Marvin (Richard Dreyfuss): *"I want some peace and quiet!"*

Bob Wiley (Bill Murray): *"Well, I'll be quiet."*

Sigmund (Charlie Korsmo): *"I'll be peace!"*

Back to the Future

Emmett Brown (Christopher Lloyd): *"Time-traveling is just too dangerous. Better that I devote myself to study the other great mystery of the universe...women."*

Honest. We even fear hummingbird attacks (woahwhatzatinmyeye). Okay, I made that one up. But I think we can agree that few things smother our joy like fear.

As a kid I lived in terror that my parents would be killed in a car accident. It paralyzed my ability to enjoy lunch, recess, and life. One day I spied a picture by my parents' bed. The text was penned in King James English: "Thou wilt keep him in perfect peace, whose mind is stayed on thee: because he trusteth in thee" (Isaiah 26:3 KJV).

Those were among the first words I ever read, yet I'm just beginning to understand them. Each time I strap myself into an airplane or lay awake wondering about tomorrow, I must remember to be a doer, not a stewer. To consciously fix my mind on the trustworthy. To cast all my care on the One who hears our prayers, knows our needs, and promises His presence. Fear paralyzes; trust mobilizes. Fear sidelines; trust strengthens. That trust will give birth to peace, and peace always leads to joy.

Worry. Bitterness. Fear. They're as useless as mud flaps on a turtle. So turn them over to God. He'll be up tonight anyway.

Trust in the LORD with all your heart;

do not depend on your own understandin

Seek his will in all you do,

and he will show you which path to take.

PROVERBS 3:5-6 NLT

If the world didn't suck, we'd all fall off.

'm fascinated by people whose lives are marked by illogical, outrageous joy—joy at doesn't make much sense. I've seen it in the lives of inmates I visit at the old folk's home, riend with bone cancer, and a resilient couple with Job-like symptoms of perseverance lid tragedy. Each has laughter that circumstances can't limit. Each demonstrates five char- teristics that together form an acronym for GRACE.

Grateful. If asked to name just one trait that lies at the heart of a healthy laugh, I would y gratitude. Two famous people impacted me in my tenth year. Only one was for good. The st was an internationally recognized minister who was speaking at a church nearby. During oast beef dinner in our home, he groused for a miserable hour about the squeaky-bed hotel which the church had placed him.

The second was Dr. Helen Roseveare. I groused too when asked to abdicate my room this skilled surgeon would have a place to stay. After all, I would miss my Styrofoam d. Though a movie was being made about her life and her books were selling briskly, she atefully gobbled a meager ham sandwich at our table and thanked me repeatedly for her imble accommodations. A ten-year-old rarely attends church willingly, but her story so ptivated me that I skipped playing football with friends to hear her speak. Raped twice iring the Simba uprising in Africa's Congo, Dr. Roseveare had survived unspeakable horror, t her words and attitude brought laughter to our home.

Gratitude is a discipline that must daily replace our sense of entitlement and our desire to side in whine country. Thankful people would rather accept than analyze, compliment than iticize. Helen Keller thanked God for her handicaps. "Through them," she wrote, "I have und myself, my work, and my God."

"Gratitude," believed Fred De Witt Van Amburgh, "is a currency that we can mint for our selves, and spend without fear of bankruptcy." Like magic, thanksgiving turns a ham sandwich into an extravagant feast, a Timex into a Rolex, and a small boy into a lifelong fan.

When I got my room back from Dr. Roseveare, two gifts sat atop my pillow, a kind note kept for years and two bucks, a veritable fortune for a ten-year-old kid.

Relational. Two guys were sentenced to solitary confinement for twenty years and allowed to bring with them only one item each. The first said, "I'll take my wife." The second decided on two thousand cartons of cigarettes. After twenty years, the first guy stepped into freedom with his wife and five kids. "We're a close family," he said. "It's been fantastic!" The second guy came out patting his pockets and said, "Hey, does anybody have a light?"

Many things go up in smoke, but well-watered relationships last. So find out who is going to cry at your funeral and hang out with them. Lower your expectations. You've never been perfect friend, so don't go looking for one. Keep secrets. Focus on what others do right. The happiest people are those steeped in community. My friend Arnold, whose wife just passed away from cancer, said, "I don't know what I would do without this church family."

Remember that a laugh is best shared, so find a way to laugh together. It's almost impossible to hold a grudge against one who makes you laugh.

Amazed. They are amazed and amused by things large and small, like sunsets, wildflowers, pets, and dryer lint. Encircled by God's extravagant creation, they seem to notice each day what others miss. Many live in a grand cathedral and spend their lives staring at the floorboards. Those who laugh best take time to look at the night sky. They listen to the questions of children and stories the elderly tell. In the laugh of a child or the roar of the ocean, they routinely hear God whisper, "Hey! I'm here. I love you."

More than anything, they are amazed by grace, by a God who says, "I will…remember their sins no more" (Hebrews 8:12). They laugh at the logic of this. A God who can number the hairs on my head yet chooses to forget my sins? A God who keeps the universe humming but keeps no record of my wrongs? This God has no taste when it comes to choosing His friends. So amazed are they that they begin to pass this grace along.

Compassionate. Never trust a dentist who hasn't had a root canal, a mechanic who hasn't been towed, or a preacher who hasn't busted his knuckles on a wrench. Pain can plant a seed deep in our soul that, when grown, produces fruit we can offer others. Joy-filled people take an uncommon interest in others. They serve. They live not to be comfortable but to comfort. Not to grab but to give. They stand out in a selfish age where we've even found a way to spell "we" with two i's.

When you're grateful and amazed, it reaches clear down to your wallet. You begin to look for needs and meet them. It makes no sense at all, but money flows to the things you love. You find yourself giving cash away at an alarming rate, knowing it can accomplish fantastic things when held in your hands but never in your heart. Tell me how you spend your money, and I'll tell you the level of your joy.

Expectant. A Sunday school teacher was testing her children to see if they understood what she'd been teaching them about heaven. "If I sold my house and my car, had a big garage sale, and gave all my money to the church, would that get me into heaven?"

"No!" the children answered.

"If I cleaned the church every day, mowed the yard, and was nice to everyone, would that get me into heaven?"

"No!" the brilliant children replied.

"Well then, if I knew all about the Bible and loved my husband, would that get me into heaven?"

"No!"

She was bursting with pride. "Well then, how can I get into heaven?"

A five-year-old boy shouted, "You gotta be dead!"

While writing this book, a man asked me this same question. Life had caved in on him when a car crash took his wife and their only child. "They believed in Jesus. I wouldn't listen…" His voice trailed off as the tears came.

I've had few greater pleasures than to point him not to a religion but a relationship with Jesus. Through simple faith in Him, we can live forever. I wish you could have seen the joy on his face as I informed him of a day that's coming when he will be reunited with his family in heaven.

Expectant? You bet. Joy-filled? Absolutely. Grateful, relational, amazed, and compassionate people overflow with hope.

THE ICE AGE

When I was five years young, I fell backward and smacked my head while ice skating. Water is hard in its frozen form, and my world went as black as a miner's lung. Protective helmets were seldom worn in those primeval times. Kids lay all over the ice, some for days. "Push Billy aside," we would say. "He's getting in the way of my slap shot."

Dad arrived, carried me home, dabbed my head with a warm cloth, and called the doctor. When I came to, he didn't lecture me on balance or explain the laws of physics by saying, "Now, sonny, gravity and clumsiness caused your head to wallop an immovable object. Your brain jangled around in your skull leaving you to languish in a post-concussive stupor."

All he said was, "It'll be okay." Then he told me of the time he passed out after smacking a lamppost. I felt so much better thinking he'd been where I'd been and believed that I could survive what he'd survived.

We all need that comfort, don't we?

As I type, my best friend, Lauren, is dying of bone cancer one room away.

Many questions nip at our heels, but his laugh is enviable, his grin a rich comfort to family and friends. Where does it come from? He'll tell you if you ask.

Beside Lauren's bed is a well-thumbed Bible telling of Jesus, the One Lauren follows. The night before Jesus died, He asked His father, "If it be possible, let this cup pass from me." On many a sleepless night, Lauren has voiced the same prayer. But in the end, with Jesus he has declared, "Not my will, but yours be done."

> **"There is One who has been here before. I can trust Him."**

His is the outrageous belief that in the midst of it all, God knows what He's up to. And that is enough. Ask Lauren what gives him comfort, and he'll tell you the same thing I thought about when my father was dabbing my head, "There is One who has been here before. I can trust Him."

Though chemo has stolen Lauren's hair, he laughs about it and asks, "What hair color does a bald guy put on his driver's license?" He has not allowed cancer to rob his hope. Cancer has invaded his body, ruined his appetite, and altered his plans, but it cannot steal his soul, cripple his faith, or change his plans for the ultimate family reunion coming one day soon.

HOW COME...

- women can't apply mascara with their mouth closed?
- no one knows what happened to Preparations A-G?
- there's never a garage for sale at a garage sale?
- drugstores make sick people walk to the back of the store to get prescriptions while the healthy buy cigarettes at the front?
- answering machines say leave a message after the beep? Can you leave one before?
- banks leave both doors open and chain the pen to the counters?
- psychics don't win the lotteries every time?

favorite fridge magnets

"Make yourself at home. Clean my kitchen."

"Therapy has taught me that it's all your fault."

"No husband has ever been shot while doing the dishes."

"Drink coffee! Do stupid things faster with more energy!"

"The house was cleaned yesterday. Sorry you missed it."

"Good friends don't let you do stupid things...alone."

"One by one the squirrels are stealing my sanity."

"They say I have A.D.D. but I think they're... Oh look! A chicken!"

"My job is top secret. I don't even know what I'm doing."

"I don't suffer from insanity. I enjoy every minute of it."

"When God was making you, He was showing off."

Our mouths were filled with laughter,
our tongues with songs of joy.
Then it was said among the nations,
"The LORD has done great things for them."

PSALM 126:2

rediscovering sanity in a mad, mad world

Even ants have time to attend a picnic.

Travel has always exhausted me. My fifth-grade teacher is to blame. She told me, "There's a bus leaving in five minutes. Be under it."

Fred Finn is the "world's most traveled man." The retired license manager has traversed the Atlantic more than 2,000 times, seen 139 different countries, visited Africa on 600 occasions, and logged over 15 million air miles (the equivalent of 31 trips to the moon and back). I don't know about you, but I'm tired just typing the last few sentences.

During a time of extraordinary stress in my life, my youngest said to me, "Dad, you don't laugh so good anymore." Few things drain laughter from our lives faster than a sped-up life, with the possible exception of flashing lights in the rearview mirror or the words "Hi, I'm your proctologist."

Writer Kurt Vonnegut said, "Laughter and tears are both responses to frustration and exhaustion. I myself prefer to laugh, since there is less cleaning up to do afterward."

A grin is a smile that blows up on us, and few things help me grin more speedily than a good comedy with Bill Murray taking baby steps onto an elevator or Peter Sellers yanking the wrong tooth. I grin when I hear Cary Grant say, "Insanity runs in my family. It practically gallops" (*Arsenic and Old Lace*). I chuckle when Steve Martin deadpans, "Some people have a way with words, and other people…oh, uh, not have way." And I laugh out loud when Martin says, "First the doctor told me the good news: I was going to have a disease named after me."

I'm told that stress contributes to ninety percent of known diseases and that we cope by ingesting 60,000 pounds of aspirin, tranquilizers, and sleeping pills per day. That's not per person, but it's still a lot.

Laughter helps, but it's not enough to provide healing and recovery. Doctors tell us that a vacation is nice, but what we need is deep rest. Soul rest. Where does it come from? When stress had me by the throat, this simple truth helped me get my joy back: *My value is not based on my performance.*

Let's be honest. The number one cause of stress is trying to impress others. We can't learn much from a two-year-old, but we can learn this: "No" is a complete sentence with a period at the end.

There is nothing noble about a nervous breakdown. For years I labored long hours thinking, *If I can just acquire or achieve, then I'll be valuable. If I can just get to the next level, people will be impressed and I'll be set.* I achieved much, but folks never seemed impressed enough. I earned much, but I was never set.

God created the earth and then rested. Not me. How could I rest? There were people awake in other times zones making money. My achievement-based identity

ook a hit when I came to see that, like God, I could be so satisfied with my work that I ould leave it alone and rest. I'm not fully there yet, but I'm learning to work because I love , not from a need to prove myself.

Nothing propels us to joy, peace, and genuine rest like knowing that God loves us, that ur sins are forgiven, and that nothing we do will earn our salvation or help us measure p. God accepts me—no, He's *wild* about me—just the way I am, not the way I should be. herefore I do what I do out of deep gratitude, which leaves me traveling light—fulfilled, ot fried or frantic.

By the way, if you're traveling to earn air miles, there's a better way. Do what David Phillips aka, the Pudding Guy) did. He calculated that the return on a mail-in food promotion utweighed the price of the frozen entrees. So he bought 12,150 individual servings of udding—for $3,140 and was awarded 1,253,000 air miles. All this while staying home.

extravagant outings for cheapskates

We all know to avoid debt, right? After all, getting into debt is like wetting the bed. It feels good for a very short period of time. So here are some priceless activities for cash-strapped, chintzy, yet adventurous souls who could use a grin.

- Eat out on Saturday. Find a friend with a Costco card and shop on sample day. Arrive just before lunch on game day and watch the big screens.
- Wash your car in the rain. Use your shirt and save laundry money.
- Revisit the VHS and 8-Track. You'll save a fortune on movies and music at garage sales.
- Pull out those old knickers and putt on the putting greens at golf courses.
- Offer to host a potluck. Have friends bring all the food.

Are you tired? Worn out? Burned out on religion? Come to me. Get away with me and you'll recover your life. I'll show you how to take a real rest... Learn the unforced rhythms of grace. I won't lay anything heavy or ill-fitting on you. Keep company with me and you'll learn to live freely and lightly.

JESUS IN MATTHEW 11:28-30 MSG

Leaving footprints worth following

Live so the preacher won't have to lie at your funeral.

Ever been at one of those funerals where you think, *Are they talking about the guy* *the casket? Am I in the wrong place?* I've been attending more funerals than I used to. After , I'm approaching fifty (I'm not telling you from which direction). If only the good die ung, what does that say about me? The other day I was looking in the mirror, and my wife pped by. I said, "Honey, I don't look fifty." She laughed. "No, but you used to." This is the dest I've ever been. I don't even know what to wear at my age. I asked Ramona if older guys ar boxers or briefs. She said, "Depends."

Ah, aging. It's not for kids. They used to ask us what we wanted to be when we grew up. one of us said, "Bald. Wrinkled. Saggy." But here we are with all this experience and in an eal position to make the most of whatever years we have left.

I've had some great examples of lives well lived. My father grew up in a crazy home where nfire and alcohol were more predictable than mealtime. He had a drinking problem. Dad ver needed glasses; he drank straight from the bottle. He saw a sign, "Drink Canada Dry," d did his very best. But God got a grip on him and altered the course of his life. Dad's gacy is one of integrity. He loved my mama for sixty-two years of marriage. His word was s bond. And he didn't chase stuff he couldn't cram in his coffin. As a result I'm the richest d in town.

Have you ever wondered how
"Don't Walk on Grass" signs get there?
Here are a few of my favorite signs:

UNATTENDED CHILDREN WILL BE given an espresso and free puppies.

Shoes are required to eat in the cafeteria. Socks can eat anyplace they want.

DO NOT DISTURB. already DISTURBED.

Gone Crazy. Back Soon.

DON'T FEED THE BIRDS. WHAT goes up MUST COME DOWN.

Procrastinate now!

SHALL i RUSH THIS jOB BEFORE i RUSH THE RUSH jOB i WAS RUSHING WHEN YOU RUSHED in?

On a maternity room door: "Push! Push! Push!"

in a pODIATRIST'S Office: "TIME WOUNDS ALL HEELS.

On a plumber's truck: "We repair what your husband tried to fix."

in a VETERINARIAN'S Office: "BACK in 5 MINUTES. SIT! STAY!"

There are at least 1,032 rewards of a life characterized by integrity. I just have space for four:

The peace of a clear conscience. Sometimes a clear conscience is a sign of a bad memory. But we all know the unsettled sense of a conscience that yelps, tormenting us when we compromise with sin. Live with integrity, and you won't have to keep your lies straight. A clear conscience gives birth to peace, peace brings joy, and joy spawns genuine laughter.

The privilege of being a mentor. When God works in your life, you have something to pass along that helps shape the lives of others.

The surprise of applause. Two high school teachers had differing approaches when it came to my plummeting marks and classroom shenanigans. The first said, "Callaway, you'll never amount to anything." The second said, "You have a gift. I want you in my Communication Arts class tomorrow morning." Guess which teacher literally transformed my life. I've had the opportunity to thank him before hundreds of thousands of people. The other teacher? I send him my books whenever they're translated into Chinese.

For the LORD grants wisdom!
From his mouth come knowledge and understanding.
He grants a treasure of common sense to the honest.
He is a shield to those who walk with integrity.
He guards the paths of the just
and protects those who are faithful to him.

PROVERBS 2:6-8 NLT

> ## "Let love and faithfulness never leave you."

The joy of a lasting legacy. We don't fixate on our legacy; we just live faithful lives. And when we're gone, our lives can still speak to those who follow.

My dad didn't leave much behind. Believe me. We have looked everywhere—sometimes with shovels! But I would take his legacy over the riches of the wealthiest of men. After all, money can buy you a house but not a home.

Though my bookshelves are filled with a thousand volumes of the finest books on faith, the person who impacted me more than any of those great authors was my mother, a simple farm girl who struggled with deep depression yet found a way to show me what it means to follow Jesus with joy.

Ever notice the names parents give their kids? Jedd I. Knight. Harry Pitts. Nice Carr. Ima Bigg. While signing books I have met Thursday, Nevaeh, and Either. (Are mothers making up names during delivery?) Proverbs 3:3-6 offers us a key to passing on the legacy of a name worth remembering: "Let love and faithfulness never leave you…write them on the tablet of your heart. Then you will win favor and a good name in the sight of God and man."

Flowery biographies adorn the web pages of authors and celebrities, but the Bible keeps its bios short. Many are just six words. God called David "a man after my own heart." Paul titled Timothy "my true son in the faith" and called himself simply "an apostle of Jesus Christ." About Jesus it was said, He "became flesh and dwelt among us."

What six-word bio would best describe you? One tombstone reads, "The richest man in the cemetery." Another reads, "An atheist. No place to go."

I think I'd like this: "Weird and wacky, yet eternally happy." Or better yet: "Traveled light. Laughed lots. Celebrated grace."

43

THE LAST LAUGH

I began this book with a story of Kurt and Lynn. Not long after Lynn bit the wrong guy, our son was bit by the love bug and fell madly in love with Kurt and Lynn's fantastic daughter. Three years later they married and forever linked us to the Cole family, a redneck band of ranchers and some of the finest people you'd ever want to meet outside a mall.

Each Christmas after shopping, they head to the woods and select the choicest spruce they can find. They trim and decorate their prize, much to the delight of Mya, the youngest of their five daughters.

Now Mya is not just any child. She's a Christmas gift herself. Adopted from China, the girl has an inspiring story and a way of getting things with a bat of her eyelashes and an upturned grin. This past year an unusual gift beneath the tree caused that grin to explode into a full-fledged laugh. It was a family trip to Mexico. Mya couldn't stop hollering and dancing and running through the house. She was about to hug palm trees for the first time in her life.

Two weeks later Mya, her face bronzed, was worried. The family was flying home during one of the worst snowstorms on record. It was a total whiteout. On the approach the aircraft weaved side to side while anxious passengers eyed the strapped-in flight attendants for signs of hope. Suddenly the engines revved, and their panic escalated. The plane surged upward, and the landing was aborted.

"This is your captain speaking (crackle crackle). There was a snowblower on the runway. We're going in for a second pass."

Rosaries were activated. Wrongs made right. A few panicked.

Though batted around like a fly in a windstorm, they went in for take two and landed with
_ _hud. Passengers could finally breathe, and Mya hollered words she'd heard at the Christ-
_as program, "Glory to God in the highest!"

Three seats away a lady yelled, "Amen!" And the plane erupted in applause.

Each January the Cole family stands their home-cut Christmas tree in a snowdrift, and
_ _en the snow melts, they prop it against the barn. Come Easter they trim the tree again,
_t this time for a very different purpose. This time they cut it into the shape of a cross.

Amid life's challenges and changes, it is the story of Easter that has given them hope.

When our son Stephen was Mya's age, we were driving past a graveyard one lazy Sunday. Noticing a newly excavated tomb with a pile of dirt beside it, the boy loudly proclaimed, "Look, Dad. One got out!"

The more I laughed at his words, the more I thought about them. And as I did, a light came on: *That's our reason for joy.* Now every time I pass a graveyard or see a cross on a chain, I am reminded that one got out. Death could not keep our Savior in the ground. Jesus Christ, the one exception to all the rules, broke the chains of death, shattered our fears, and promised eternity with Him.

> **The more I laughed at his words, the more I thought about them.**

A man once asked me, "What's the funniest joke ever?" I have no idea, but here's a good candidate. I was walking past the asylum, and I heard the inmates chanting, "Thirteen, thirteen." I looked through a hole in the fence, and some idiot poked me in the eye with a stick. I walked away, and they chanted, "Fourteen, fourteen."

If you hear me snickering and wonder why, I just may be thinking about that joke, some goofy quote, or Lynn's surprise attack in the mall. But bankrolling it all will be the laughter of a guy who knows the greatest punch line in all of history—God loves a guy like me. Like a kid who can barely tune his oboe and gets to play with the London Philharmonic, I've been shown so much grace that I can't stop grinning. Like a girl who has little chance of survival and gets a home, an extravagant trip to Mexico, and Easter too, I've encountered hope that rises like yeast under the warmth of God's love.

We don't know what's around the next corner, do we? But we do know this. We are loved beyond reason, blessed beyond belief—and free to laugh.

*The most thoroughly wasted of all days
is that on which one has not laughed.*

NICOLAS CHAMFORT